Ten Poems about Puddings

ex libris

Candlestick Press

Published by:
Candlestick Press,
DiVersity House, 72 Nottingham Road,
Arnold, Nottingham NG5 6LF
www.candlestickpress.co.uk

Design, typesetting, print and production by DiVersity Creative
Marketing Solutions Ltd., www.diversitymarketing.co.uk

Illustrations: © Rosalind Bliss, 2009
Introduction: © Nigel Slater, 2009

© Candlestick Press, 2009
Reprinted 2010, 2011, 2012

ISBN 978 0 9558944 7 3

Acknowledgements:
The publisher acknowledges with thanks Cathy Grindrod for
permission to print 'How To Make Apple Crumble', Alexander
Hutchison and Salt Publishing for permission to print 'Surprise,
Surprise' from *Scales Dog*, Salt Publishing, 2007, Bloodaxe Books
and each respective author for permission to print, 'Preamble' by
Julie O'Callaghan (*Tell Me This Is Normal*, Bloodaxe Books, 2008),
'How to cut a pomegranate' by Imtiaz Dharker (*The Terrorist at My
Table*, Bloodaxe Books, 2006) and 'Forever Afters' by John Agard
(*Alternative Anthem: Selected Poems with Live! DVD*, Bloodaxe Books,
2009) and Grevel Lindop and Carcanet Press for permission to print
'Summer Pudding' (*Tourists*, Carcanet Press, 1987). Special thanks to
Nigel Slater for his Introduction, which in our view earns him the title
of Pudding Laureate, and to Sally Meech for her research.

Introduction

Pudding...pudding...pudding. A word so full of joy and comfort, a word to solve problems and soothe every ill. It's a word to make you celebrate.

I'm not sure there isn't a crisis that couldn't be helped with a dish of bread and butter pudding. It can mend a broken heart and silence a screaming child, end an argument and say 'I'm sorry'. I sometimes wonder if it might actually stop a war. It might be worth a try.

I wouldn't mind living on syllabub, flummery and pie. (Just as long as I could have syrup sponge now and again.) And I have yet to come across anything, anywhere in the world that is quite as nice as warm treacle tart and cream.

Pudding is what we all really want when we are down or unhappy. It cheers us and keeps us going. It sets us up to face the world. It can alter our mood too: there is something ultimately settling about a bowl of rice pudd or a round of roly-poly, just as there is something uplifting about a bowl of trifle or a knickerbocker glory.

I have always felt that eating pudding is rather like being in love. Only better. Just saying the word makes you feel happy. Try it.

Nigel Slater

'Blessed be he that invented pudding'

Henri Misson
*Memoirs and Observations of Travels
Over England, 1719*

Forever Afters

Served, as always, for the last.
The tail end of the menu.
The main course's epitaph.
A pudding knows the meaning
of waiting one's turn in queue.
Patience is what puddings know best.
And when all face the final test
on that day of reckoning,
puddings will array their glory
down to the smallest gooseberry,
for every pudding knows one truth –
that the first shall be last
and the last shall be first.
Yes, puddings shall have the last laugh
when the sweet inherits the tooth.

John Agard

How to make Apple Crumble

Balance in your palm a green winter moon.

Slide a steel blade in
  to set in motion
  the fall of spiralling skin
  wheeling in rings,
  twisting its light path,
  splashing a snake-trail on marble.

Slice your naked moon.

Let flour rain
  like dust motes through sun beams
  in kitchens of glass.

Make a sweet blanket,
  rough as a cottage, pebble-dashed;
  where a witch once lived
  who stirred a spell in an earthenware dish
  the colour of sand.

Smother your slivers of apple moon
  like a fresh snowfall.

Make it white hot.

Take a cold spoon;
  dig deep to its creaking core.

Cathy Grindrod

At a Dinner Party

With fruit and flowers the board is deckt,
    The wine and laughter flow;
I'll not complain – could one expect
    So dull a world to know?

You look across the fruit and flowers,
    My glance your glances find. –
It is our secret, only ours,
    Since all the world is blind.

Amy Levy, 1889

Summer Pudding
for Carole Reeves

Begin with half a pound of raspberries
picked from the deep end of your sloping garden, where the birds
   play hopscotch in the draggled fruitnets; add
a quarter of redcurrants; gently seethe in orange juice
   for six or seven minutes with some sugar,
giving the pan a ritual shake from time to time, inducing
   a marriage of those fine, compatible
tastes; and leave to cool. An open kitchen door invites
   whatever breeze will help itself to flavour,
attenuating it downhill across your neighbours' gardens
   (be generous!) so summer will surprise them,
an unidentifiable recalled fulfilment haunting
   the giant bellflower and the scarlet runners.
Now introduce your strawberries, sliced to let the pallid heartsflesh
   transfuse its juice into the mass, transmute
cooled fruit to liquid crystal while you line your bowl with bread
   and add the mixture – keeping back some juice –
lid it with bread, cover and weight it, chill it if you like
   (as if the winter took a hand) and hoard it,
opus magnum ripening its secret, edible,
   inviolable time. And when you dare
slide your knife round its socket to uncling – a sudden suck –
   this gelid Silbury mined with the wealth
of archetypal summer, let it be on one of three
   occasions: for a kitchenful of children
whose mouths grow purpleringed and flecked with whipped
     cream as they dig
   and lose, entranced, the treasure of the minute;

or for the friends around your polished table, when that soft
   lake of mahogany reflects the faces
melting in candlelight and burgundy, rivers of talk
   eddying to a stillness lost in taste
primitive as a language, clear as thought; or for whoever
   will join you in your garden when the sun
carries out summer to the edge of dark, and stay to eat
   there in the early chill as twilight gels
and owlhoots quiver from the gulf of darkness, where a floodlit
   cathedral floats under your eyes, and still
(wreckage of smeared plates and clotted spoons piling the table)
   after the lights are killed and the cathedral
vanishes like a switchedoff hologram, remain to plot
   the moon's progress across the brimming air
scaled by the nightscented stocks, or with binoculars
   arrest the Brownian movement of the stars.

Grevel Lindop

Surprise, Surprise

MacSween the corner butcher with confidence displays
for denizens of the city – 'of toons the *a per se'* –
a vegetarian haggis, rank specimen of his craft.
Just what the creature might contain defeats surmise:
pinmeal and onions, nuts or beans, some dribs and drabs.
No gristle, no suet, no organ meats: no liver, no tripes
no lights, no heart. Instead of a sheep's paunch
potato skins with a saddle-stitch fly. Up the Mound
down Candlemakers Row the fix is in. The makars jump
the peddlers stump, the market splits wide open.

First *from a purely culinary point of view*–corned, curried
devilled, smoked and kosher haggis; haggis à la king; wee
cocktail haggis; haggis in a basket; haggis on the half-shell;
instant haggis; English haggis; haggis eclairs; Crimean
campaign haggis, conceived in Sebastopol, consumed in
Balaclava; hot-cross haggis; haggis in plum sauce; dessicated
haggis; baked haggis alaska; chocolate mint-chip haggis;
non-stick convenient haggis; cucumber and haggis
sandwiches; junk haggis; whole-hog haggis.

Next *by haggis of a special bent*–weight-watcher haggis;
haggis for the moonstruck; haggis *nouveau*; haggis *grand
cru*; 12 year old vintage haggis matured in oak casks; 100
year old Kung Po haggis drawn from the well without
obstruction; "Bomber" Haggis; haggis for lovers;

lite, lo-tar, lo-nicotine haggis; Campdown haggis; drive-in haggis; hand-raised, house-trained haggis, with pedigree attached; haggis by special appointment; reconstituted haggis; nuclear-free haggis; ancient Dynastic haggis sealed in canopic jars; haggis quickstep; haggis high in fibre; haggis low in the opinion of several discerning people; a haggis of the Queen's flight; Nepalese temple haggis (rich, dark and mildew-free); hard-porn haggis; haggis built to last.

Finally *objects tending to the metaphysical*–desolation haggis; the canny man's haggis; haggis not so good or bad as one imagines; haggis made much of caught young; unsung haggis; haggis not of this fold; haggis dimm'd by superstition; perfectly intuited haggis; haggis beyond the shadow of a doubt; bantering haggis; haggis given up for Lent, haggis given up for lost; haggis so good you think you died and went to heaven; haggis supreme; haggis unchained.

Alexander Hutchison

Preamble

Mary Fran, Kathy, Lizzy,
my own dear cousins, for that you did
transport me to Dairy Queen
and there repeatedly force me
to eat hot fudge sundaes;
and also, that at your premises on Pratt Avenue
you did compel me to partake of
chocolate chip cookies
and brownies under false pretences.
You may be seated.
Jack and Rosemary, my misguided parents,
that you did, on numerous occasions,
lure me against my will into eating houses,
to wit, Poppin Fresh Pies, Town and Country,
The International Pancake House, Dunkin Donuts,
Mario's Italian Lemonade Stand, among others
and did wantonly thrust sundry items
of food in front of my face.
Next, please.
Kate, Ellen and Nora, siblings, you also
did cause me to procure Hostess Twinkies,
onion pizzas, popsicles,
Arby's Roast Beef sandwiches,
bagels and cream cheese.
The aforementioned are the principal
defendants in this case
but I must also indict my mouth
for aiding and abetting them
in the corruption of my body.
The court may rise.

Julie O'Callaghan

Untitled

O for a roly-poly Mother used to make.
Roly-poly, treacle-duff,
Roly-poly that's the stuff.
Only to think about it makes my tummy ache,
O Lor' lummee! I wants my Mummee
And the puddens she used to make.

Anon

Pease Pudding

Pease pudding hot,
Pease pudding cold,
Pease pudding in the pot,
Nine days old.
Some like it hot,
Some like it cold,
Some like it in the pot,
Nine days old.

Anon

How to cut a pomegranate

'Never,' said my father,
'Never cut a pomegranate
through the heart. It will weep blood.
Treat it delicately, with respect.

Just slit the upper skin across four quarters.
This is a magic fruit,
so when you split it open, be prepared
for the jewels of the world to tumble out,
more precious than garnets,
more lustrous than rubies,
lit as if from inside.
Each jewel contains a living seed.
Separate one crystal.
Hold it up to catch the light.
Inside is a whole universe.
No common jewel can give you this.'

Afterwards, I tried to make necklaces
of pomegranate seeds.
The juice spurted out, bright crimson,
and stained my fingers, then my mouth.

I didn't mind. The juice tasted of gardens
I had never seen, voluptuous
with myrtle, lemon, jasmine,
and alive with parrots' wings.

The pomegranate reminded me
that somewhere I had another home.

Imtiaz Dharker

The Christmas Pudding

Into the basin
put the plums,
Stir-about, stir-about,
stir-about!

Next the good
white flour comes,
Stir-about, stir-about,
stir about!

Sugar and peel
and eggs and spice,
Stir-about, stir-about,
stir-about!

Mix them and fix them
and cook them twice,
Stir-about, stir-about,
stir-about!

Anon